PANDAS

WILDLIFE IN DANGER

Louise Martin

Rourke Publishing LLC
Vero Beach, Florida 32964

www.rourkepublishing.com

PHOTO CREDITS:
Cover Photo© Lynn M. Stone

EDITORIAL SERVICES:
Pamela Schroeder

Library of Congress Cataloging-in-Publication Data

Martin, Louise, 1955–
    Pandas / Louise Martin.
        p. cm. — (Wildlife in danger)
    Includes index
    ISBN 1-58952-020-3
    1. Giant Panda—Juvenile literature. 2. Endangered species—Juvenile literature.
        [I. Giant Panda. 2. Pandas. 3. Endangered species] I. Title

QL737.C214 M3384 2001
599.789—dc21

                                                                    00-067073

Printed in the USA

TABLE OF CONTENTS

GIANT PANDAS

The giant panda is China's best known and most popular wild animal. It is also one of the world's most **endangered** wild animals. Endangered animals are in danger of becoming **extinct**. Extinct animals are gone forever, like the dinosaurs.

Scientists believe that fewer than 1,000 wild giant pandas remain. Another 140 live in zoos.

The lesser, or red, panda is not a close cousin of the giant panda

The giant panda is in the bear family, but it is a most unusual bear. Unlike other bears, giant pandas live almost entirely on a plant diet. And they rarely eat any plant except bamboo.

The lesser, or red, panda shares the panda name, but it is not a bear, nor is it a close relative of the giant panda. The lesser panda is related to raccoons.

Fog hides evergreen trees in a Chinese mountain forest where giant pandas live

WHERE GIANT PANDAS LIVE

Giant pandas live only in the **provinces** of Gansu, Shaanxi, and Sichuan in southwestern China. Giant pandas live in cool, rugged mountain forests that have dense stands of bamboo. Giant pandas in summer may hike upward to almost 13,000 feet (3,900 meters) above sea level. In winter, they move downhill, sometimes into forests just 2,600 feet (800 meters) above sea level.

Giant pandas live almost entirely on a diet of bamboo

GIANT PANDAS IN DANGER

China has more people than any other country. For every person in the USA, China has about four. With so many people, China has turned many of its forests into farms and villages. Giant pandas and other wild animals have had fewer and fewer places to go.

Giant pandas have disappeared from at least five provinces during the past 2,000 years. China's growing human population has been the main reason for the loss of giant panda **habitat**, or living space. But changes in climate have also reduced panda habitat.

Giant pandas sometimes climb a tree and nap among the branches

There are many different kinds of bamboo

A panda in its natural habitat

In addition to loss of habitat, pandas have often been shot for their fur and body parts. Ancient Chinese folk medicine believes that wild animal parts can cure a variety of human ills.

Few pandas are shot today, but the condition of their habitat is a problem.

The furry coat of a giant panda keeps it warm in snowy weather

GIANT PANDA FOOD

For animals with the teeth of **carnivores**, or meat-eaters, giant pandas have a strange diet. A giant panda can eat over 25 pounds (11 kilograms) of bamboo in a day. And much of a giant panda's day—up to 14 hours—is spent munching on bamboo leaves and stems.

Giant pandas must have bamboo forests to survive. Fortunately, in 1998, China stopped nearly all tree-cutting in giant panda habitat.

Most of the world's 140 captive pandas are in Chinese zoos

SAVING GIANT PANDAS

China does not have a long history of protecting wildlife or its habitat. For most Chinese, wild animals have been used for food, clothing, or medicine. Protecting giant panda habitat from logging, then, is a giant step forward for China.

In recent years China has changed in many ways. One change has been a much greater interest in saving endangered wildlife, especially the giant panda. China has made strict laws against killing giant pandas. Between 1985 and 1991, China sentenced three **poachers** to death. Several other poachers were given life in prison.

Adult giant pandas weigh up to
350 pounds (160 kilograms)

China has new programs to raise giant pandas in captivity. Baby pandas are very difficult to raise, but the Chinese have made great progress. Captive pandas may some day be released into safe, wild habitats.

Giant pandas take few vitamins from bamboo, so they must eat huge amounts of it

Meanwhile, in another change, China has welcomed help from Western countries like the United States and England. Two of the most active groups in giant panda **conservation** are the World Wildlife Fund and the Zoological Society of San Diego. With worldwide help, China may be able to save its wild giant pandas.

GLOSSARY

carnivore (KAR nuh vore) — a meat-eating animal, such as a tiger

conservation (kon sir VAY shun) — the careful, planned saving of land, water, plants, or animals

endangered (en DANE jerd) — to be in danger of becoming extinct

extinct (ex TINKT) — having disappeared altogether; no longer existing

habitat (HAB uh tat) — the certain type of place where an animal naturally lives, such as a rain forest

poacher (PO chur) — one who kills animals that are protected by law

province (PRAH vintz) — any one of several regions in China, similar to American states or Canadian provinces

INDEX

	DATE DUE	